THE STORY OF THE HOT DOG

Text & Illustrations Copyright © 2022
Historical Kids Books
ISBN: 978-1-959319-01-6

Written & illustrated by Madeline Rivers.

The story of the hot dog begins in 1841. When a very special boy named Charles Feltman was born in Germany.

Charles hated using forks.
Charles hated using spoons.
Charles even hated using knives.

He would always ask, "Why do I need to use a fork, when I can just use my fingers?"

"Why do I need to use a spoon, when I can just drink my soup from the bowl?"

"Why do I need to use a knife, when my teeth are plenty sharp?"

His mother reminded him, "If you don't use silverware, you will get food and grease all over your hands and your clothes. You wouldn't want to ruin your clothes now, would you?

"You're right mama." Said Charles. "But when I grow up, I'm going to move to America and I'm never going to use silverware again!"

And then in 1856, that's what Charles did.
He left his home in Germany and moved to
New York City, USA!

Charles was ready when he got to New York. He had brought as many frankfurters and sausages as he could carry.

"People in America will love my real German sausages. I bet that they will line up around the block to buy my frankfurters." He thought.

But when he got there, he couldn't believe his eyes. Sausage shops of the finest quality, and on every corner! "Who will buy my sausages now?" He thought.

"Oh, how could I have been so wrong?
What ever shall I do?" worried Charles.

So Charles kept walking.

And walking...

And walking...

And then in 1867, he passed a bakery
and saw some oddly shaped
buns for sale.

"Ah Ha! I've got it!" Charles jumped in the air with excitement and went running into the bakery.

"I would like to buy all the buns you have!"
Charles said to the baker.

"Young man, may I ask what you are planning to do with all of these buns?" asked the baker.

"Come to my food cart tomorrow in Coney Island and you can see for yourself."
Said Charles.

The next day the baker went to the
food cart. And by golly, there was
a line around the block!

Charles had put the sausages he brought from Germany inside the buns. Now people could eat with their hands without getting grease on themselves.

He called his new creation,
the Coney Island Red Hot.

People. Went. Crazy!

They started eating red hots at baseball games.

They started eating red hots at football games.

People ate red hots at the beach.

People ate red hots at carnivals.

"Red Hot Dogs! Come get your Red Hot Dogs!" could be heard everywhere. But after a while, the name was shortened to Hot Dog.

People loved eating hot dogs so much,
they started having contests to see who
could eat the most!

Since it was created, people's love for the hot dog has never faded.

It holds a special place,
in our hearts and on our plates.

And just one bite,
will bring a smile to your face.

Although we may never know,
what exactly is in it.
One thing is for sure,
they are always delicious.

We have Charles Feltman to thank.
He sure was clever.
And the world will keep loving
hot dogs forever and ever.

More stories about your favorite foods

Shop Historical Kids Books.com

Made in the USA
Las Vegas, NV
09 October 2023

78850148R00021